So, You Want to Be Anointed?

The Anointing Equips You for Ministry.

Patricia Jones Taylor

Copyright © 2014 by Patricia Jones Taylor

So, You Want to Be Anointed?
The Anointing Equips You for Ministry.
by Patricia Jones Taylor

Printed in the United States of America

ISBN 9781629524283

All rights reserved solely by the author. The author guarantees all contents are original and do not infringe upon the legal rights of any other person or work. No part of this book may be reproduced in any form without the permission of the author. The views expressed in this book are not necessarily those of the publisher.

Unless otherwise indicated, scripture quotations are taken from the King James Version of the Bible.

www.xulonpress.com

Table of Contents

Acknowledgements vii

Words from My Husband and Apostle xv

Foreword xvii

Introduction xix

Chapter I	Understanding the Anointing	23
Chapter II	Process of Being Anointed	27
Chapter III	Signs of the Anointing	35
Chapter IV	Making Full Proof of the Anointing Through Testing	37
Chapter V	A Message to Christian Parents	50
Chapter VI	Knowing Your Children's Enemy	55
Chapter VII	Backlash	61
Chapter VIII	Anointed in Your Living, Giving and Worship	67
Chapter IX	Anointed to Preach, Called to Pastor	73
Chapter X	Advantages to Being Anointed	83
Chapter XI	Commonly Asked Questions about the Anointing	85

Conclusion 87

ACKNOWLEDGEMENTS

Very special thanks to our Intercessors who stayed on the wall travailing on our behalf. We are eternally grateful for your love through your works. Thanks for covering us through the completion of this Book. The attacks were great, they formed but they could not prosper because you guys stood in the gap with us. Thanks for being qualified help. James 5:16

Prophetess Candace Collier	Ministers Rosevelt & Alpha Copeland (II Kings 3:11&12)
Pastor Lisa Langie	Bishop Daniel & Pastor Terryle Parker
Pastor Anthony F. Eaton	Bishop Demetrics & Pastor Pauline Roscoe
Pastors Leon & Linda Lee	Ministers Allen & Roselyn Jones (Jones Family Prayer Line)

Thanks to our four children: Elijah, Elisha, Victoria, Jesse and our Grandson Jeremiah DeWayne Taylor. You guys mean the world to us. I believe one of the reasons God gives pastors children is because He knows through them we will always have an illustration in our messages. There is never a dull moment with you guys. Children will guarantee you a prayer life. Your Dad and I see all of you somewhere in your future and you look much better than what you look right now. Love you, eternally.

Special thanks to my mother, Mrs. Melville Jones, who has been blessed to live upon this earth and in good health for the past 87 years. I Love you Mom and I thank God for you.

Much gratitude to our family members, all of my eight living siblings, nieces, and nephews: Bessie Jones McMillan, Marilyn J. Lane,(Antone) Doris J. Richardson, Rallis Bro, (Bettie), Lawrence & Allen Jones(Roselyn), Angela Jones Cotton, Niece Lanye Webb (James), Niece Jamese Toyer. Thanks for your part in my making that has birth the anointing in my life. I have witness such spiritual growth in each of you. Confrontation is not always bad when it runs the recipient in the presence of God. Thank you family, You guys have help to develop my love walk. I Love My Family.

Special thanks to my youngest sister Rhonda (Eugene), who, as many of us, God has on the potter's wheel. He is making her meat for the Master's use and His alone. Thanks Renaye for all the love and support that you give to our children and others. You are often misunderstood by your actions, but You indeed have a servants heart. Trust God and obey. God gives seed to the sower and bread for food and He multiplies your giving. Giving is Gods way to Prosperity. Greater is Coming!

Special thanks to Cousin Kay Williams, God placed in mine and Elisha's life in a very transitional time. Thanks for hearing God's voice

ACKNOWLEDGEMENTS

and obeying in initiating Jones Family Prayer Line on Monday nights. Many lives have been changed for the better because of it. Thanks Kay.

Thanks to our Cousins Kerry and Carolyn Gibson, Brother Lawrence Jones and two of our church members who volunteered to take our son, Jesse into their home until he came through the fog. But God had his route already sketched. Thank you for being willing to make a difference.

Special Thanks also to Cousin Greg and Latoya Winn, for calling daily to check on his cousins and to offer assistance. Thanks Greg for being there as a Brother and friend for your cousin when He needed you most.

There will always be a special place in our heart for Aunt Susie Crumb. Her legacy of love and service to mankind lives on in the lives of her family. Thanks to Uncle Herman, Cousins Andy (Gwen), Toby (Tammy), the children and Northside Christian School Family. Also thanks to Aunts, Mary Winn & Aunt Stein.

Thanks to those of you who were there with encouraging words and special help whenever we called for your assistance. Thanks to three special people who were a part of my foundation of development spiritually, who took me under their wings and their home and showed me God through their love and support: Godparents and Pastors Alfred and Mary Joyce Williams and special childhood friend, Patsy Caddell Wehby.

Special Thanks to our spiritual godchildren Bishop Daniel & Pastor Terryle Parker, who truly loves their Heavenly Father and us. Not just in words, but in deeds. Thank you for the continuous bountiful Blessings. You are blessed to be a blessing. We thank God for your obedience.

Minister Adam Goodman, who stood faithfully with us until his appointment. He shall be restored to us soon. Adam, this too is the trying of your faith. Our God is faithful and He will set you free to your ministry. Be encouraged and know the anointing will carry you through to destiny.

Minister Tammy Goodman, a true servant at heart. Thanks Tammy for believing in us and standing with us through service. The scripture states a faithful man or woman shall abound with great Blessings. You have been there and made the sacrifices to serve us whether through styling mine or Victoria's hair or preparing a meal for us or the ministry and never expecting anything in return. You have seed in the ground, expect your harvest.

Thanks to special friends through the years. Pastor Edward Kirkland, Evangelist Cynthia Hall, Sister Yvette and Mariah Sims, Sisters Marie Arnold, Cecelia Mitchell, Amelia Grier, Shelly Walker, April Williams, Michelle Avery, Stacey Allen and the list goes on.

Special Thanks to our spiritual godchildren Ministers Damon & Jennifer Graham, Minister Joe Evans, Minister Bonnie Brown and children, Minister Yvaughn Pierce, Brother Jerry and Austin Pugh, (Son) Reynard Gulley, Sister Danielle Chester and the children, Sister Kim Carlisle and the girls, Sisters Deanna & Desiree Pugh, Sister Sherill Latham, Sister Yinlustra Gordon and Mother, Sister Melanie Long, Sister Pam and Devoy Thomas, Ministers Kerry & Ashley Harmon.

ACKNOWLEDGEMENTS

Very Special Thanks to Dr. Edward O. Jackson, (Sister Marilyn) Pastor Greater New Antioch Baptist Church. God knows his name. God spoke to His servant and he obeyed. Pastor Jackson asked few questions, made no demands but responded with Answers. Thank you Pastor, for hearing the voice of the Good Shepherd and obeying. Eternally Grateful.

Special thanks to Family and Special Assistants, Book proofreaders & editors: Minister Viola Broadnax & Sister Sharon Howze. Who can find a friend who will stick closer than a Brother or Sister? God has given us such in these two vessels. The Blood of Jesus has caused our relationship to be just as close as any natural kinship. These sisters, not just on this project but through the years have been there for us, in spirit and in truth. Thank you again Viola and Sharon for the love and the countless hours you spent being patient with me while I deliberated the book contents several different times. True love is patient and it is kind. Thanks sisters for being Kingdom minded through this process.

So, You Want to Be Anointed?

Thanks to those who contributed financially to help get this message out to the body of Christ:

Elders Frank & Bonita Brown	Ministers Anthony & Kimberly Eaton
Ministers Rosevelt & Alpha Copeland	Bishop Daniel & Pastor Terryle Parker
Brother Eugene & Sister Rhonda J. Warren	Minister Timothy King
Minister Faynita London & Children	Brother Theo & Sister Adrienne Nichols
Sister Sharon Howze	Pastors Alfred & Viola Broadnax

HIS WORD Ministry Family, we are presently small in number But huge in power. We are close knitted through God's Word. Thanks for standing with us through this process of being Anointed. You are an amazing group of people and we love you for it.

H.E.R.S. (Honoring Every Resurrected Sister). We thank God for this ministry He birth in me over twelve years ago. We meet every second Saturday of each month at 11:00 am at the Church. Thank you Sisters for grabbing the vision and running with it that we may bring healing and hope to every Resurrected Sister. (If you are not connected, please join us)

Special thanks to the Teachers and Staff at Thompson and especially Carver High School for your indulgence with my dear children

ACKNOWLEDGEMENTS

and especially Jesse. Your patience and going the extra mile with Jesse, helped to bring longevity to my life as well. Thanks for seeing Jesse, not as he appeared but in his purpose. Thanks to all of you, for your encouraging words that his actions are only temporary. Bless you as you continue to educate and make a difference in the lives of our young people. Educators are ministers for God, continue to walk worthy of your calling.

From the Heart of My Husband and Apostle

The word says he who finds a wife finds a good thing and obtains favor from the Lord. I found that favor and more when God blessed me with this anointed vessel and Daughter of Zion. It has been an honor to grow in the things of God with her as we together have experienced awesome moves of God. Our lives have been greatly enriched through the study and application of the Word of God. We have seen God's faithfulness to us in many circumstances and situations that has only caused us to trust and love Him more, as well as each other.

This Book is written out of that growth in Him. So as you read this Book it is our prayer that you will be encouraged and seek Him to know His Will concerning being anointed.

What a powerful subject matter, though sometimes misunderstood amongst the Believers. This Book is timely as we enter the season of our Lords return. The True work of the Ministry can only be accomplished through being anointed. Just as Jesus was anointed; we too have to be anointed to be that extension of him in the earth. People are thirsty for a demonstration of the Holy Spirits power; signs Wonders and miracles follow the anointed word when preached. The body of Christ must travail again until the true anointing that sets a man free, rest in the Body again. We have seen enough of flesh. It is time to pay the price to see the Glory of God.

I encourage every believer to search out the truth concerning being

Anointed. The anointing is not for fame or fortune but healing and deliverance.

When we get anointed we will fulfill the work of Christ in the earth. He said

Greater works than these shall you do, in the earth also. It will not happen without the anointing. Within these pages this truth is revealed. Read with an Open ear to hear what the spirit is saying. Pay the price to be anointed.

M. W. Taylor Apostle

FOREWORD

*P*astor Patricia has done it again, allowing Creator-God to order her steps to produce another delightful and enlightening work. She defines anointing by negation. This approach seems best since we are in a world that seeks to define God's terms by its own carnal and limited understanding. Pastor Patricia readily renounces the world's views of anointing and extols the Biblical view. Though she boldly shows what the anointing is not, she humbly, yet powerfully, shares what it is, using examples from her own life, family, church, and beyond. She lucidly identifies demonic strongholds and how to wield the "sword of the Spirit" as the believer's weapon of victory to surmount every imaginable opposing force. If you've ever wondered about whether God has called you to serve and what it takes to be effective, or if you've not taken heed to His call because of a lack of understanding of how He empowers those He calls, then So You Want to be Anointed? is a must read. It will challenge you to discover your place in the Body of Christ and to serve faithfully, and it will also prepare you to take the journey – with patience – the Lord has charted for you. What will it take to transcend the ordinary and to break the chains of the enemy? The Anointing! So You Want to be Anointed? My answer is YES! What's yours?

Pastor Anthony F Eaton
Kingdom Mission Church
Raleigh, NC

Introduction

*I*n American churches today, one may frequently hear these expressions, "I am anointed", "the anointing fell on me" or "he is really anointed". How many really understand what it means to be anointed? Because one has the ability to play an instrument well, sing well, or preach eloquently does not mean the anointing is present in his life. To better understand this word, and how it relates to individuals and corporate gatherings, one must look to the scriptures to find out the intent of the Heavenly Father when it relates to ministry gifts. All ministry gifts should be anointed and work in harmony one with another.

Christians should earnestly desire to be anointed. There is nothing wrong with this. In fact the bible tells us:

> The yoke is destroyed because of the anointing
>
> (Isaiah 10:27b).

> How God anointed Jesus of Nazareth with the Holy Ghost and with power; who went about doing good, and healing all that were oppressed of the devil, for God was with him
>
> (Acts 10:38).

One could conclude from the scriptures referenced above that being anointed is an honorable thing as long as you have the right motives. The purpose of the anointing is to turn people to Jesus, to lead them to Him in repentance. It also brings about deliverance in the lives of those that are bound. However, one must admit that many want the anointing in order to draw people to themselves, satisfied with the mere appearance of being able to remove someone's burden and yoke from off their neck. They believe if they are anointed, they will have a large following. They will live in a large house within a gated community and drive a Lexus or Mercedes Benz. The anointing has been reduced to merely praying for someone and seeing them fall out with no real deliverance taking place. The truth is demonic spirits are still manifesting and sin is present. God does not entrust His anointing to His ministers to bring them fame and glory. It is for His glory and His alone.

The anointing is not the same as being talented. One may identify an individual or group on *Sunday's Best*, *Dancing with the Stars* or *American Idol* as being anointed. While this is a possibility, it is not necessarily true. They are talented. They are gifted or graced to perform. Having gone to programs at various churches, I have witnessed extraordinary talent as the artists ministered on stage. What was disturbing, was after one particular performance these same artists, who were described as being anointed, did not display behavior consistent with the lifestyle of one who was submitted to God. These men went outside and pulled out their cigarettes. They began to talk about going to the club to meet up with women. Other ungodly conversations followed. We must understand God's anointing abides in sanctified vessels.

"For the gifts and calling of God are without repentance" (Romans 11:29). You can have a gift or talent to sing, dance or shout and still be in sin, on your way to hell. You can attend church and still be in sin. These acts can be performed without salvation.

An individual can be talented due to skill or family genes. If one's mother and aunts are all singers, that talent could be inherited by that individual. It is not uncommon. One could be a great athlete because his granddad, dad and uncles are all great at sports. Talents are given by God and can be passed down through the bloodline, but one cannot inherit the anointing. When a Christian says he wants to be anointed, he desires the yoke destroying, burden removing power of God in manifestation in his life. This is truly a great thing, but it comes with a cost. Anything of value has a high price tag that might not be immediately visible, but will be revealed.

Chapter I

Understanding the Anointing

The anointing is the ability or power to stand up under extreme pressure and have joy in the midst of sorrow. It enables you to keep a positive outlook when things seem dark. You understand that God is bigger than the problem you are facing. It is the ability to love your spouse when he/she seems unbearable; the ability to resist having pre marital sex even when your body is craving. The anointing is the declaration and certification that you have met the standards of approval and acceptance of the Father, Son and Holy Ghost. The anointing is the apex of a Believers walk with God.

According to the **Merriam-Webster Dictionary**, to anoint is defined as to smear or rub with oil or an oily substance. **Strong's number h8081** defines the term anointing as shemen; fat or oil; a feast of fat things; and the yoke (of Israel) is broken because of fatness," a metaphor taken from a fat bull that casts off and breaks the yoke, "And it shall come to pass in that day, that his burden shall be taken away from off thy shoulder, and his yoke from off thy neck and the yoke shall be destroyed because of the anointing" (Isaiah 10:27).

In the Old Testament, the priest was given oil to smear upon those who were chosen to be a mouth piece of God. This oil represented the presence of God upon their life. Also kings in the historical narratives could officiate at the sacred altar like a priest, after being smeared with the sacred oil. Moses, for example, transferred the anointing (by hand laying) upon a ru'ah-endowed Joshua (Numbers 27:18-20). However, in the New Testament, Jesus introduces His church to the Holy Spirit. It is no longer oil poured over an individual that displays the presence of God upon his life. Neither is it the laying on of hands by man. We have the Holy Spirit that guides and teaches us as we go through life's trials. As we follow His lead He will produce fatness or the oil to bring about deliverance, not only to ourselves, but others as well.

After a believer's faith is tried as by fire through tribulation, distress, persecution, famine, nakedness, perils or sword, his reward is seen through the anointing. Just as fire purifies precious metals in the earth, the fire of the various obstacles mentioned above begins a purification process in the believer's heart. God becomes magnified in his eyes, heart, and life, and then his faith grows. He trusts God all the more, and now God's desire is to use the believer to set others free. God's anointing flows through his life, and his ministry is validated with signs, wonders, and miracles: "And these signs shall follow them that believe (or anointed); In my name they shall cast out devils; they shall speak with new tongues. They shall take up serpents; and if they drink any deadly thing, it shall not hurt them; they shall lay hands on the sick, and they shall recover" (Mark 16:17).

When we are tested and tried as by fire, we too can come through with praise, not even smelling like smoke. The three Hebrew boys, spoken of in the book of Daniel, illustrate this perfectly: "And the princes, governors, and captains, and the king's counselors, being gathered together, saw these men, upon whose bodies the fire had no power, nor was an hair of their head singed, neither were their coats changed, nor the smell of fire had passed on them" (Daniel 3:27).

The anointing will cause others to come to know your God. After Shadrach, Meshach and Abednego endured their trial, King Nebuchadnezzar spoke:

> "Then Nebuchadnezzar spake, and said, Blessed *be* the God of Shadrach, Meshach, and Abednego, who hath sent his angel, and delivered his servants that trusted in him, and have changed the king's word, and yielded their bodies, that they might not serve nor worship any god, except their own God. Therefore I make a decree, That every people, nation, and language, which speak anything amiss against the God of Shadrach, Meshach, and Abednego, shall be cut in pieces, and their houses shall be made a dunghill: because there is no other God that can deliver after this sort. Then the king promoted Shadrach, Meshach, and Abednego, in the province of Babylon" (Daniel 3:28-30).

Again, how you go through your trial will determine what you will come to. The Hebrew boys steadfast faith brought souls to the kingdom. The same thing occurs with us today. Our being steadfast through our testing will be a witness to the lost. The anointing will reveal to you and others who you are in God. The power you possess through the Holy Spirit will allow you to hold up under extreme pressure.

The anointing terrifies our adversary. He recognizes that he is no match against it. The anointing is the burden removing, yoke destroying power of God in manifestation. True believers are anointed, and then appointed.

Chapter II

Process of Being Anointed

The **first step** to being anointed is **salvation**. One must have **a relationship** with God the Father, Jesus the Son and the Holy Ghost. The bible states "these three bear record in heaven, the father, the Word and the Holy Ghost; and these three are one" (1 John 5:7). The difference between talent and the anointing is relationship. The scripture implies that God is the source of the anointing. As the source, one must be plugged in, having a relationship, in order to receive Him:

"Jesus answered and said unto him, "Verily, verily, I say unto thee, except a man be born again, he cannot see the kingdom of God" (John 3:3).

The **second step** to being anointed is receiving **the Baptism of the Holy Ghost**, as Jesus did.

> And John bare record, saying I saw the Spirit descending from heaven like a dove, and it abode upon him (Jesus). And I knew him not; but he that sent me to baptize with

> water, the same said unto me, Upon whom thou shalt see the Spirit descending, and remaining on him, the same is he which baptizeth with the Holy Ghost. (John 1:32-33).
>
> But ye shall receive power, after that the Holy Ghost is come upon you; and ye shall be witnesses unto me both in Jerusalem, Judea, and in Samaria and unto the uttermost part of the earth. (Acts 1:8).

Many times we want the end result without going through the process. Understanding the process and the prerequisites required to receive what we are asking for, determine the end results. When Jesus told his disciples they were going to the other side to do ministry, he did not tell them what would come before they actually reached the other side.

> And the same day, when the even was come, he said unto them, Let us pass over unto the other side. And when they had sent away the multitude, they took him even as he was in the ship. And there were also with him other little ships. And there arose a great storm of wind, and the waves beat into the ship, so that it was now full. (Mark 4:35-37)

Jesus did not tell the disciples the storm was coming, and many times we do not know when we are headed for a storm. Nevertheless he provides us with the help we need to get through the storm successfully; the Holy Spirit:

> "And I will pray the Father, and he shall give you another Comforter, that he may abide with you forever"
>
> (John 14:16).

> "But the anointing which ye have received of him, abideth in you and ye need not that any man teach you; but as the same anointing teacheth you all things, and is truth and is no lie, and even as it hath taught you, ye shall abide in him"
>
> (1 John 2:27).

To be anointed one must be submitted completely to the Lord. Jesus is our perfect example. In the Garden of Gethsemane, he prayed, "…Nevertheless, not my will, but thine, be done" (Luke 22:42).

The **third step** to being anointed is **character development**. You must allow the word of God to dwell in you richly to bring about the necessary changes to be made useable. Change is inevitable in the life of a Believer. The Saints of old termed it as, I looked at my hands and they looked new; then I looked at my feet and they did too. What a wonderful change that has taken place in my life, since I allowed Grace to place me in my assignment. The bible states in Romans 12:2, "And be not conformed to this world: but be ye transformed by the renewing of your mind, that ye may prove what is that good, and acceptable, and perfect, will of God. Your gift or talent can carry you where your character can't keep you. God's anointing rests upon vessels of integrity.

The **fourth step** to being anointed is **having a prayer life**. Prayer is another essential attribute to the anointing. Prayer is a spoken or unspoken address to God. It is communication with Him. The scripture tells us that we are to pray: "I would therefore that men pray everywhere lifting up holy hands" (I Timothy 2:8); "Men should always pray and not faint" (Luke 18:1 b).

If you want to be anointed, if you want to be in the will of God, you must live a life of prayer and fasting. Paul states in Galatians 4:19 "My little children of whom I travail in birth again until Christ be formed in you". Christ here refers to the anointing also. In prayer the anointing is birth that empowers you to endure during your testing, even through a report of sickness or disease your faith will not be moved. Even if a threat of job layoff or even a house or business foreclosure, your emotional state of being, will be at peace,

You must be sold out to God's will, which is the word of God. It is interesting that, even with Christians, prayer is not something we readily embrace. People will come to programs, musicals, and recitals, but not many will come out to prayer meetings to pray. Those that do come, become fidgety after fifteen minutes. Their mind starts wandering toward their "to do list". Satan is wonderful at his job of bringing all non-kingdom related "to do lists" to your remembrance when God is at work in your life. His objective is to remove your peace and to increase worry and anxiety. Satan's intent is to cause you to focus on past experiences; what you do not have, who you owe, something mean a person said to you or about you. The goal is to disturb your peace. In prayer we are reminded that Jesus is in control and we are to cast all of our cares and concerns on Him. Prayer keeps you in your hour of temptation: "Could you not watch with me one hour? Watch and pray that you enter not into temptation; the spirit indeed is willing, but the flesh is weak" (Matthew 26:40-41).

You must have a consistent prayer life in order to house the anointing. What you do privately, God will reward publically: "When you pray enter into your closet, and when thou hast shut the door, pray to the Father which is in secret; and thy Father which seeth in secret shall reward thee openly" (Matthew 6:6).

Prayer is not optional to be anointed. It is a mandate. There are at least four divisions of Prayer that bring God's presence on the scene:

1. Worship (the highest form of Prayer). Adoration of His Deity. (Psalms 100) Enter Into His Gates/ Presence with Thanksgiving.
    a. Note: When we enter His Presence with Praise, He enters our circumstances with Power.
2. We are to make our request known. (Mark 11:24) & (Philippians 4:19)
3. Put God in remembrance of His word, what He has promised. (Philippians 4:19)
4. Pray in the Spirit/our heavenly language. Identified by many as the Holy Ghost (Romans 8:26 & 27).

The **fifth step** in being anointed is **fasting. You must fast:** "Moreover when ye fast be not, as the hypocrites, of a sad countenance, for they disfigure their faces, that they may appear unto men to fast. But thou, when thou fastest anoint thine head, and wash thy face" (Matthew 6:16).

Fasting is when you choose to abstain from pleasure, whether food, activities, people, to seek the face of God. It is a major component of the anointing. If an individual struggles with saying "no" to food, he will also struggle saying "no" to gossiping, unforgiveness, fornication (whether homosexual or heterosexual), adultery, pornography, drugs, alcohol, coffee, sodas and ungodly conversations. The disciples asked Jesus "Why were we not able to cast it out?" (Matthew 17:19b) This question was posed to Jesus after He had cast an evil spirit from the son of a man who had come seeking Jesus for his son's deliverance. He had initially taken the boy to Christ's disciples, but they were unable to cast the demon out. Jesus' response was, "howbeit this kind goeth not out but by prayer and fasting" (Matthew 17:21). Fasting deflates the flesh and inflates the spirit.

"Know ye not, that to whom ye yield yourselves servants to obey, his servants ye are to whom ye obey; whether of sin unto death, or of obedience unto righteousness?" (Romans 6:16).

If you feed your spirit the word of God, it will grow and dominate; but if you spend more time feeding your flesh, it will expand and dominate. Keep in mind that in our flesh dwells no good thing. That's why we should seek to crucify, put to death, our flesh and bring our spirit man to life.

For our spirit was created in the likeness of Jesus. Even Jesus, being our example, fasted for 40 days. Nothing crucifies our flesh like fasting. We should live a fasted life; a life whereby we say "no" to sin and unrighteousness and "yes" to the will of our heavenly father. Fasting is your earnest money (a mortgage term) whereby the potential buyer gives a down payment to show the seller that he is committed to buying the house. He is not just talking, he is making an investment. He is a serious buyer. Fasting tells the Lord that we are serious and committed to our request and we prove this by giving up that which means a lot to us for a season. Fasting is not optional to be anointed. It is a mandate.

Chapter III

Signs of the Anointing

"And these signs shall follow them that believe; In my name they cast out devils; they shall speak with new tongues. "They shall take up serpents; and if they drink any deadly thing, it shall not hurt them; they shall lay hands on the sick, and they shall recover." (Mark 16:17)

This scripture indicates the signs of the anointing that is revealed in the ministry. There are also character signs that will promote an individual into ministry. They are listed below:

1. **They are faithful and committed** – "The same commit thou to faithful men, who shall be able to teach others also. Thou therefore endure hardness, as a good soldier of Jesus Christ" (II Timothy 2:2-3). They are "steadfast, unmovable and always abounding..." (I Corinthians 15:58).

2. **They have unconditional love** – "Charity suffereth long, and is kind; charity envieth not; charity vaunteth not itself, is

not puffed up, Doth not behave itself unseemly, seeketh not her own, is not easily provoked, thinketh no evil; Rejoiceth not in iniquity, but rejoiceth in the truth; Beareth all things, believeth all things, hopeth all things, endureth all things" (I Corinthians 13:4-7).

3. **They are sanctified, set apart and marked** – "Nevertheless the foundation of God standeth sure, having this seal, The Lord knoweth them that are his. And, let everyone that nameth the name of Christ, depart from iniquity. If a man therefore purge himself from these, he shall be a vessel unto honor, sanctified, and meat for the master's use, and prepared unto every good work" (II Tim. 2:19).

4. **They have great faith** –They fight the good fight of faith, lay hold on eternal life, whereunto thou are also called, and hast professed a good profession before, many witnesses" (I Tim 6:12); **They have the God kind of faith** – "Now faith is the substance of things hoped for, the evidence of things not seen" (Hebrews 11:1), "…calling those things that be not as though they were." (Romans 4:17)

5. **They are peculiar and unique to their purpose and call** – "But ye are a chosen generation, a royal priesthood, an holy nation, a peculiar people; that ye should shew forth the praises of him who hath called you out of darkness into his marvelous light"(I Peter 2:9).

Chapter IV

Making Full Proof of the Anointing Through Testing

"But watch thou in all things, endure afflictions, do the work of an evangelist, make full proof of thy ministry" (II Timothy 4:5).

"And Jesus being full of the Holy Ghost returned from Jordan and was led by the Spirit into the wilderness (to be tested) of the devil for forty days" (Luke 4:1).

Many times in life we make our requests to God in prayer, not knowing what we have to go through to receive what we have asked for. God knows what is needed to bring about the results, just as He knew that part of His disciples training for ministry would involve preparation for dealing with storms. We claim to want worldwide ministries, but again, the qualification of being anointed is being willing to pay the price to be convinced that Jesus is real. There was a song that my mom used to sing, as she did the housework. It was one of her favorite songs entitled, "My God Is Real, for I Can Feel Him in My Soul". She would often talk about knowing God through the hard times. After birthing and raising nine children, she came to know God as her provider. Truly going through will bring you to a place called "convinced". Convinced can be defined as "sold out in the thought realm, no negotiation, fully persuaded, verdict is in, no reasonable doubt. As in a court of law when the verdict is reached, the jurors are convinced that the evidence presented is factual; can be substantiated.

True anointing is not taught, but caught through dying to self and service to another who is anointed. Elisha received the anointing of Elijah through commitment and service to the prophet:

> And he said, Thou hast asked a hard thing; nevertheless, if thou see me when I am taken from thee, it shall be so unto thee; but if not, it shall not be so. And Elisha saw it, and he cried, My father, my father, the chariot of Israel, and the horsemen thereof. And he saw him no more: and he took hold of his own clothes, and rent them in two pieces. (II Kings 2:10,12)

> And one of the King of Israel's servants answered and said, here is Elisha the son of Shaphat, which poured water on the hands of Elijah. And Jehoshaphat said, the word of the Lord is with him. (II Kings 3:11-12)

King Jehoshaphat knew that Elisha was anointed because he had been the faithful servant to Elijah, whose anointing was known throughout the land.

The anointing is also caught through "crushing" or "wounding". Wine is made through the crushing of grapes; olive oil is made through the crushing of the olives. Gold must go through the fire to remove impurities that devalue it. Being anointed comes about from being crushed, splattered, and then dissembled in order to be made all over again. Anything and all things of value come forth after being proven. Pressure causes you to truly see what is in you, good and bad. In the life of a believer, it allows them to identify what they truly believe in God's word and what they do not. For example, if you put enough pressure on any given object you can break it into two or more pieces and define its contents. Even when broken, a believer's ability to stand is based on the amount of God's Word in his heart. This breaking process is also known as dying to the flesh. The bible states it like this:

> Verily, Verily, I say unto you, except a corn of wheat fall into the ground and dye, it abideth alone, but if it dies it brings about much fruit. He that loveth his life shall lose it; and he that hateth his life in this world shall keep it unto life eternal. If any man serve me, let him follow me; and where I am there shall also my servant be; if any man serve me, him will my father honour. (John 12:24-26)

> And the vessel that he made of clay was marred in the hand of the potter; so he made it again another vessel, as it seemed good to the potter to make it. (Jeremiah 18:4)

> But the anointing which ye have received of him abideth in you, and ye need not that any man teach you; but as the same anointing teacheth you of all things, and is truth, and is no lie, and even as it hath taught you, ye shall abide in him. And now, little children abide in him; that, when he shall appear, we may have confidence, and not be ashamed before him at his coming. If ye know that he is righteous, ye know that every one that doeth righteous is born of him.
> (I John 2:27-29)

A little clarity, note that the anointing does not rest upon a believer because they merely do right most of the time, but they live a life of righteousness, just as Jesus.

There is a cost to the anointing. It is truly an individual merit. The anointing is not based on a group effort nor can it be a class assignment. The anointing comes as the believer experiences trials:

> That the trial of your faith, being much more precious than of gold that perisheth, though it be tried with fire, might be found unto praise and honour and glory at the appearing of Jesus Christ. Whom having not seen, ye love; in whom,

though now ye see him not, yet believing, ye rejoice with joy unspeakable and full of glory; Receiving the end of your faith, even the salvation of your souls.

(I Peter 1:7-9)

The Lord graced me to remember that Job's anointing was validated after he survived his storms:

> And the Lord said unto Satan, Hast thou considered my servant Job, that there is none like him in the earth, a perfect and an upright man, one that feareth God, and escheweth evil?... And there was a day when his sons and his daughters were eating and drinking wine in their eldest brothers house: And there came a messenger unto Job, and said, The oxen were plowing, and the asses feeding beside them; And the Sabeans fell upon them, and took them away; yea, they have slain the servants with the edge of the sword; **and I only am escaped alone to tell thee.** While he was yet speaking, there came also another, and said, The fire of God is fallen from heaven, and hath burned up the sheep, and the servants, and consumed them; **and I only am escaped alone to tell thee.** While he was yet speaking, there came also another, and said, The Chaldeans made out three bands and fell upon the camels and have carried them away, yea and slain the servants with the edge of the

swords; **and I only am escaped alone to tell thee.** While he was yet speaking, there came also another, and said, Thy sons and thy daughters were eating and drinking wine in their eldest brother's house: And, behold, there came a great wind from the wilderness, and smote the four corners of the house, and it fell upon the young men, and they are dead; **and I only am escaped alone to tell thee…** In all this Job sinned not, nor charged God foolishly.

(Job 1:8, 13-19, 22)

Job trusted God. Even though he did not understand what was going on, he knew that God was righteous. He had enjoyed the blessings that God had bestowed on him, so his thoughts were that he had to accept the bad along with the good. He did not realize that God had placed him as an example before Satan.

Satan's goal was to prove that Job did not really love God but only served Him because of the family, material possessions and health that God had bestowed upon Job. "However, put forth Thy hand, now, and touch his bone and his flesh; he will curse Thee to thy face" (Job 2:5). God, by allowing Satan to attack Job, proved to Satan that Job indeed loved Him and was willing to trust Him in the midst of his storm. Job got to know God better and actually received knowledge from God during his ordeal. Job asked God a series of questions that proved God has knowledge of things that man does not have or even understand. Job was able to stand the test. He was blessed after the ordeal, but that ordeal is what brought about a new revelation of who God is. All of Satan's attacks brought Job into a closer walk with God.

We have come to understand that our attacks come because God is preparing us for the journey He has ordained us to travel. Based upon the scriptures we just read, Job was tested in four major areas: character, wealth, health and family.

Job's character was on trial. He was described as, blameless, upright, fearing God and turning away from evil; however, when he was being tested, those closest to him questioned his integrity. They immediately resorted to attacking his character to find weaknesses, flaws or areas of sin. His friends felt that there had to be sin in his life. They did not realize that God had ordained the circumstances to illustrate that Job would not charge God foolishly.

Many times we too have found ourselves in situations, wondering why we are experiencing such hardships. We had to conclude that this was an ordained test of God to prove our love and devotion to Him, through trials of our faith.

Job lost his wealth. Satan asked God the question, "…Does Job fear God for nothing?" (Job 1:9). Satan challenged God to allow what God had blessed Job with to be taken away and then see that his (Job's) true love was for riches. Many serve God for what His hand can provide, not for His presence. Job lost all of his wealth through his oxen, donkeys and servants, but Job proved that his devotion to God was based on their relationship, not on God's resources. As with Job, we too have suffered the loss of cars, houses and even a business that had to be closed.

Job was tested in his health. "And Satan answered the Lord and said "Skin for skin! Yea, all that a man hath will he give for his life. But put forth thy hand, now, and touch his bone and his flesh, he will curse Thee to Thy face.... Satan went out from the presence of the Lord, and smote Job with sore boils from the sole of his foot to the crown of his head" (Job 2:4-5, 7). As with Job, Satan is still speaking today. He is challenging God concerning His people saying, that if God allows sickness or death of a love one to occur, that we will stop serving Him. Through having a relationship with God, we understand that God has the power over death, hell, the grave and sickness; and healing is a benefit to salvation. We must not get into fear but faith. God can use sickness, **even death**, to show His power. He called Lazarus forth from the grave after he had been dead for four days. God has the final say on our outcome.

God blessed me to write my first book, **"Life's Not Over Until God Says It's Over"** in January 2011. In it, I shared my testimony of how God miraculously spared my life after suffering a massive heart attack. If you have not had a chance to read it, I highly recommend that you do so. **In my previous book, I tell of my "out- of- body" experience.** When one thinks about the phrase "out-of-body", one could relate it to something spooky or ghostly. Most times no matter where I am when I start sharing my testimony that my spirit came out of my body, there's a holy hush that comes across the audience. Only our Heavenly Father can take a man or woman's spirit out of his/her body, and there still remains life.

I went to the hospital on Christmas Day 2009, experiencing chest pains. After having several tests done, I was told that I had had a massive heart attack and that I needed emergency surgery but procedure could be fatal. I was also told if I did not have the surgery, my heart would stop because four of my six arteries were completely blocked. So having a relationship with the Father, He gave my husband and me peace concerning having the surgery. Having an agreement in a marriage is so important. Now while on the operating table, the Father took my spirit out of my body and allowed it to hover over my body while time stood still. I actually saw my body being operated on. In mid air, I ask the question," how could I be in two places at the same time?" Then my spirit was transported to Judgment Day. I was in a court room setting. There was a trial taking place that involved me. There I was being tried to determine if I would continue to live on earth or go on to my eternal resting place. I know many of you have watched the television show "It's supernatural" with Sid Roth, but this actually happened to me. Most of his guests live in exotic places out of state, in another country or on an island somewhere, but this encounter happened to a lady who, at the time, lived in Alabaster, Alabama.

The prosecuting attorney revealed my sins committed while in the body. Be reminded that your sins one day will testify against you. When my Defending attorney began to present my case, he told the Judge, representing Jesus, that all of my sins are now under the Blood and in no court of law can you try a person twice for the same offense once the price has been paid. Because I have an acceptable relationship with the Father, I was granted permission to live on until the Rapture (The coming of the Lord). I admonish you to live a repentant life. The good news is if you die in right standing with the Father, your faith will testify in your favor that the price for His children's redemption has already been paid on Calvary through the shedding of Jesus blood. Isn't that good news?

My spirit then went back into my body on the operating table and my heart continued to beat. God showed me something else. He said that He stands outside of time determining time. Hear me with your spirit. He said man is governed by time, but He set time. I asked Him, "What do you mean by that?" He said take your surgery for example, the average heart rate is 72 beats per minute at rest, and zero point eight three, three per second. Between those minutes, I can hold the beats still until I finish making a man or woman, I can perform surgery, I can determine the verdict of a court hearing and judgment outcome between the two beats. He said a thousand years with man is as one day before me. He that has an ear to hear what the spirit just revealed let him hear.

My mandate was to go back to the earth and remind man and woman that Jesus is on his way back, "Be Ready!" It is now going into the fourth year since my surgery and God has indeed proved to be faithful. I plead with you religious and/or sinner man to look around you and observe the times. Get a Relationship with the Father while you still have time so you can have the power to stop sinning, and, therefore you will, " be ready" upon His return.

Job was also tested with his family. Job offered sacrifices to God daily on behalf of his children in case they had sinned and cursed God in their hearts. He lost all of his children. When his health began to go downhill, Job's wife said to him, "Do you still hold fast your integrity? Curse God and die!" (Job 2:9). Many times Satan will use those closest to you, your family members, when they don't understand who you are in God, to challenge your peace or to be a distraction from your assignment. Even as Jesus prayed, "Lord forgive them for they know not what they do". We too have to pray for our family members for God says when they do it to the least of mine; they do it also unto me Matthew 25:45. Our family members must know they can not deal with Gods anointed as with kindred flesh, But as the servant of God.

One of the miracles that God performed in my life was blessing me with my children. When my husband and I married, I was told that I would not be able to have children. This was unacceptable to us. I have been an educator all of my adult life and I have a heart for children. I knew that God would honor my desire for children. My husband and I got in agreement and began to believe God for our children. It was not an easy or glamorous road, but in the end God blessed us with four beautiful children.

So, You Want to Be Anointed?

Now, here we are, finally getting three of our four children off to college. I thought that my youngest son would be rejoicing. He was about to experience the ideal life of being the only child at home. No more sharing the television remote, rooms, or anything. He would even have all of mom and dad's attention. However, instead of embracing this time, the adversary manifested his presence in my youngest son. He began to act out by shutting down and going into his own world. Even before the others left, he began rebelling. I had stated earlier, there were very drastic changes that took place in our lives and he did not adjust well to them.

We had to move to a different area of town. He stated that he did not like his new school. He stopped playing his instrument at church and his dress changed. He started to wear loud, uncoordinated clothing. He took little or no interest in his appearance. To be honest, it seemed as though the only person at home he would have any interaction with was my middle son when he would come home from college. He seemed to want to identify with him. At this time, we were experiencing problems with this son as well.

Chapter V
A Message to Christian Parents

This Chapter may not be readily received by everyone. Referring back to book title, "So, You Want to Be Anointed?" this entire book is for that select group who wants to do it God's way. Christian parenting comes with a high price tag, but God's power through the Holy Spirit has made it affordable. We must admit that there are parents out there whose main objective is to be their child's best friend and be accepted by them. We must all first come to the realization we don't know how to parent. We copy our parents. Yes! There were a lot of things they may have done right and if they would be honest there were a lot of things they did wrong. Without the Holy Spirit leading, we too will miss it big time. If you are not open to truth, you may not endorse this chapter. Only those of you who still desire to raise your children according to scripture that they may have long and a fruitful life will get excited. We want you to know "You are not a lone ranger", and that there are still others out here that will not compromise truth either.

A Message to Christian Parents

"And let us not be weary in well doing; for in due season we shall reap, if we faint not" (Galatians 6:9). There is a lie that we must dispel in the earth. Fathers teach your sons how to do drugs and drink responsibly because they will all do it. Mothers put your daughters on birth control pills because they all will experiment with sex. We cannot buy into the myth that "all children raised in a Christian home will rebel". I have witnessed the fear upon many parents of how their children will turn out if they train them up the bible way. Everybody has a story that goes like this, "I knew somebody's children who went astray in a Christian home because the parents were too strict on them". Yes, this might be true, but they fail to say for every one story where the child went astray due to Christian values, there are five stories to be told of children being imprisoned or killed due to lack of enforcing Christian principles in the home. I would prefer any day having the privilege of seeing my child go astray and come back compared to never returning due to not being instructed or compromising. True, chastening or correcting in the mind of a child means no freedom to explore.

We must keep in mind that Satan is the god of this world and that he has strategically assigned some of his demonic spirits in human bodily form to befriend your child. Why? To cause them to want to be accepted and to be made to feel that they are in charge of their own lives through deception. One lie is that you, their parent, do not want them to enjoy their life. You are trying to control them and prevent them from having fun; having a life. The truth is we, as parents, want them to live to be able to have a life. Our children are being told that drugs help you to feel good. You need them to be able to relate because they give you an escape from this confusing world of rules and restrictions. All of this is a lie. Another one is that sex with altering partners, even the same sex, is healthy and this is a way of showing how we think for ourselves. We are our own person and therefore we won't be dictated to or controlled.

A child, as early as the age of 8 (third grade), could begin to show signs of this spirit starting to try and seed them with their independence. They tend to want to start detaching from their authority:

1. **In their interests**. In their entertainment and music, they suddenly need privacy. They will begin to wear ear plugs, head phones, start closing their bedroom doors. When you enter their space, as they refer to it (**mind you, in your own home**) you will hear "Mom, you didn't even knock"!
2. **In their dress**. If you pick out or suggest one outfit, if they wear it, they will find some way to alter your suggestion. In their mind, they are sending a message that they did not obey you completely and therefore they are in control of their life.
3. **In everything.** Even in their seating at home or away they want to put distance now between you and them to send a message to you and others who may see them, "I do my own thinking". If they are made to come to church, they want to sit in the back, and rebel through their posture making a statement, "I am here

but I won't willingly participate. My parents are Christians but I never told anyone that I was. I'm doing me."

Parents, we cannot buy into the lie that this is the fate of our children and this is a "lost generation". We can't be moved by what we see. We must walk by faith. We must speak to the mountain:"For verily I say unto you, that whosoever shall say unto this mountain, be thou removed, and be thou cast into the sea; and shall not doubt in his heart, but shall believe that those things which he saith shall come to pass; he shall have whatsoever he saith" (Mark 11:23).

We as Christian parents must choose to believe the report of the Lord. God's report says in the book of Proverbs:

> Foolishness is bound in the heart of a child; but the rod of correction shall drive it far from him. (Proverbs 22:15)

> Chasten thy son while there is hope, and let not thy soul spare for his crying. (Proverbs 19:18).

> Remove not the old landmark; and enter not into the field of the fatherless; For their redeemer is mighty; he shall plead their cause with thee. (Proverbs 23:10-11)

This last verse is counseling to Christian parents. Do not try to revert to "new school" training in raising your children. The instruction of the old landmark is still applicable today. God's word never loses its proven affects. His Word does not need to adjust to the times, for the times are in His hand and therefore the times, years, adjust to His Word. When you as parents do the Word concerning raising your children, your heavenly father, as in a court of law, if necessary will be your lawyer, witness and judge. We must keep in mind we are living in a time where people are calling wrong right, and right wrong. The mindsets of the masses are influenced by television talk shows and Hollywood celebrities. In such cases as portrayal of the family unit, one man to one woman has become obsolete. You are told that in order to adjust to the times you have to be liberal in your thinking and open minded. Today's interpretation of that is two men raising a child, two women, or a woman can just get pregnant by a man and raise the child without him.

Galatians 4:27 states, "For it is written, Rejoice thou barren that bearest not; break forth and cry, thou that travailest not; for the desolate hath many more children than she which hath an husband." Something indeed is wrong with that picture. America has forgotten her God and therefore judgment will be released upon a wayward and disobedient people.

Christians, we must trust our heavenly father for our desired results in our children. My husband and I realize first hand, through raising our four children that standing for the right thing will bring on a fight of rebellion with our children. It became even more real to us nearing the conclusion of this book.

Chapter VI
Knowing Your Children's Enemy

And they went into Capernaum; and straightway on the Sabbath day he entered into the synagogue, and taught. And they were astonished at his doctrine; for he taught them as one that had authority, and not as the scribes, And there was in the synagogue a man with an unclean spirit; and he cried out Saying, Let us alone; what have we to do with thee, thou Jesus of Nazareth? Art thou come to destroy us? I know thee who thou art, the Holy One of God. And Jesus rebuked him, saying, Hold thy peace, and come out of him. And when the unclean spirit had torn him, and cried with a loud voice, he came out of him. And they were all amazed, insomuch that they questioned among themselves, saying. What thing is this? What new doctrine is this? For with authority commandeth he even the unclean spirits, and they do obey him. (Mark 1:21)

So, You Want to Be Anointed?

What new doctrine is this? Interesting question huh? There is a new doctrine that targets our youth. It has been released through music and videos known as the Luciferian doctrine. Parents, you may want to note that our children are pulled into a self-initiated doctrine whereby they are instructed to be in control of their own life- "I'm setting out to make me happy". Not only to make their own decisions, but also to be the captain of their fate. Even if their decision is not logically sound or in their best interest, their mindset is still to show that they are in authority, and they are in control. The other question this spirit causes them to want to present is, "What makes you feel that your God is the only God? Don't I have a right to choose who I want to serve?"

The spirit that was using my son would cause him to sit in church with ear plugs in his ear, refusing to take them out. Other times he would come to church but refuse to come into the sanctuary. Any person in authority who attempted to address his behavior was responded to with complete defiance. We had asked a social worker, who was a friend of the family, to talk with him. He refused to cooperate. She was the first one to diagnose him with ODD (Oppositional Defiance Disorder). It was later confirmed again by others assigned as his caseworkers. Again, we knew that this kind would only come out through "fasting and prayer". We are convinced that God's word is true and therefore we will see the deliverance power of God in manifestation in all of our children's lives. God cannot lie and "He will perfect that which concerneth me…" (Psalms 138:8).

God had given us to start prayer around the altar on Monday nights at the Church. True as the saying goes, a new level spiritually qualifies through a new level of devils. We have concluded that the devil only fights what God is about to advance. On Monday evenings the men and women would gather at the altar and travail until the presence of God manifested, destroying the power of bondage or addiction in their lives. Many of our members would bring their coworkers or family members for prayer and God would break every chain in their lives as well. In this God would heap coals of fire on our adversary. In turn, he (the adversary) began to heighten his attacks against us. His target became our children, the most vulnerable links. The weapons formed against the oldest three but we prayed them on through. He (Satan) remembered we had one last son at home, so he decided to target him for his arsenal of mass destruction here. I can imagine how he called a meeting of the satanic minds together and threatened them and gave an all out bulletin request, "not to let this one escape". The more we ministered, others were saved and delivered. The more our son manifested defiance against our authority at home.

We went home one day after a great service and our son had cut off his eye brows. His only response of why was, "It's my body and I should be able to do with it as I please". We can imagine how Jesus felt when he was mocked while he was hanging on the cross, "He saved others, let him save himself" (Luke 23:35).

God spoke to me and said this kind comes out only through prayer and fasting. We would ask to pray for him and he would refuse. Be

So, You Want to Be Anointed?

mindful, this is our youngest son. The one that was most mild mannered and he and I spent the most time together. He had gotten to the place if he came to the church, he would not come in service. He would stay downstairs or go outside. He got to the place where he would not get his hair cut, not even trimmed. He said to us that all of his life others have told him what to do, now he is only going to do what he wants to do. He had become totally defiant. A note to parents, if you have raised a teenager or have younger children, you already know or will know that most of them go through a temporary state of insanity, maybe not medically diagnosed but through observation. They can't or they refuse to seek an understanding of the changes that take place in their body and mind during their development. In turn, they shut the authorities out or they become hostile or quick tempered toward them. Good news, they will eventually come through it.

This was very difficult for my husband and me. It is very hard to experience an onslaught of Satan, especially when it involves someone you love. Many times what the adversary's plot is for saints to look at one another according to the flesh and not see him (Satan) lurking behind or inside that individual. It's not your supervisor, coworker, church members, children, spouse, parents, or sibling. It is Satan using them to affect your emotions. His assignment is to disturb our peace and joy, to cause us to see the outcome in a negative way, and to expect the worst in every scenario. We found out the most effective way to defeat Satan, is to do "good" toward mankind. Love those who despiteful misuse, abuse and lie on you because Satan has no defense against your love. Love weakens his attacks and destroys his power.

This was not my son, but an evil spirit that was on an assignment to torment my husband and me through him. Satan had given his demons the assignment to become a distraction to us so that we would not focus on our assignment. **Remember your attacks come many times because of the assignment.** If Satan can not stop us, he will try to delay us. Be encouraged in knowing that "delay does not denote denial". Although we might become delayed through distractions or postponed through being perplexed, our struggles develop our strength. Satan knows that parents love their children and that they would go to any extent to provide, protect and promote the future of their children. The bible says, "If ye then, being evil, know how to give good gifts unto your children; how much more shall your heavenly father give the Holy Spirit to them that ask him?" (Luke 11:13).

Children are God's inheritance and it gives Him great pleasure to give His children the Kingdom. God's Word states "no good thing will he withhold from them that walk uprightly". Psalms 84:11 The children of the Kingdom have been made in His image and likeness. Just as it is in the natural, so is it in the spirit. Parents love their children and therefore will put their own lives in harm's way for them. Satan realizes that if he wants to disarm a man or woman who is doing serious damage against his kingdom, he will find a way to kidnap or enslave their children or other love ones. In our case, it got to the place that every Sunday the fight would be on. Satan would use our son to try to draw us out from our peace or assignment. But we were steadfast and unmovable to our assignment, so that we could abound in the anointing.

Chapter VII

Back Lash

We had a powerful two-day Prayer Explosion, "War Cry", at our Church. We called for the five fold, the Apostles, Pastors, Prophets, Evangelist, Teachers and all who were called to intercede. We prayed according to II Chronicles 7:14-15 which states, "If my people, which are called by my name, shall humble themselves, and PRAY, and SEEK my face, and TURN from their wicked ways; then I will hear from heaven, and will forgive their sin, and will heal their land. Then my eyes shall see you, and my ears will hear your prayers."

We prayed for three straight hours, both days. We called down principalities, powers, rulers lurking in dark places, seducing spirits, compromising, lying, deceit, hypocrisy, doctrines of devils, jezebel (rebelling, controlling) spirits, homosexual, gay, lesbian spirits, abortion, murdering spirits, satanic occults We tore down the altar of Baal worshippers, and every spirit that exalted itself against the knowledge of Christ.

We prayed especially against those unclean spirits that has been loosed and assigned to our young people. Their assignment was to destroy them by convincing them to violate the Word of God whereby they would not honor (respect) their mother and father, so their days would not be long upon the earth.

After the two day meeting, we began hearing many testimonies of deliverance. We knew we had done much damage to the kingdom of darkness, but the confirmation came from our very own son.

Our youngest son went into a very combative mode with us, even to the point of challenging his dad. The devil had plotted to have a death occur in our home that morning but our heavenly father covered us. He showed us the weapons formed, but they did not prosper. Our ministering angels were on post. God had directed us to start a fast a week prior. The Holy Spirit woke us up around 6 am the morning of the occurrence, to pray and begin worshipping. We had no idea what was about to go down. A Word to the spiritual, when God say pray, Pray! We didn't know what all to pray about. We prayed in the Spirit (Holy Ghost) and allowed our spirit to pray about what would take place (Romans 8:26 -27). In most cases your obedience can result in the life of someone you know being spared. Obedience is better than any sacrifice, so by all means don't allow anyone to deceive you. If you don't have a prayer language, given by the father, please get with another believer and ask them to pray with you to receive the Holy Ghost. (Luke 11:10-13) You will need Him!

My husband had instructed my son to get up for school. He refused to. Can you believe that, a child telling a parent "no". In our day, we wouldn't have dared to say "no" to our parents. If we would have tried it, we would have been looking around the room for our teeth and some of our other body parts. My husband tried to reason with my son and not give any place to Satan. As on many other occasion when my son would defy him, the apostle in him, would try to deal with him logically and with love. I would be in the back ground brewing, because it was nine of us and some of us, mind you, might have needed to be on some medication, but by the time my dad finished beating us, we got real good sense and got healed. (lol). So I know if it worked for us, and none of us ever went to jail or prison or ended up in a hospital for something foolish, it would work for our children and grandchildren. We got beat, not for talking back, but looking like we thought about wanting to talk back.

My son decided to take my husband on, God had instructed my husband that this was a spirit in manifestation. So he began to rebuke the evil spirit and continue to deal with it spiritually and all of a sudden my son got in his face and hit him. My husband indeed retaliated back against our son and hit him with an object but the angels intervened and only allowed him to scrape the side of his head. God said He did not give us over to the will of our enemy. Serve God and He will take care of you. We called the police and told them what had happened. Because our son was a 17 year old minor as they termed it; not considering his size, disrespect, or the fact that he passed the first lick, and because my husband drew blood when he hit him, they arrested my husband for hitting a minor. I was outraged. A man should have the right to defend his house and family, even if against his own child. We felt as though the system had failed us. We had tried on several occasions to get the system to get involve but they wouldn't until this occurrence took place.

The real fight began here. My husband was carried to jail and my son was being seen by a physician. I was told that either my son or husband could return to the house but not both of them. Imagine that! The adversary began to throw darts against my mind like never before. I was in one the worst fights of my life mentally. The accusation from the adversary was I should have done more. We had failed as parents. I had to come home to an empty house and the adversary knew it. He seized the moment to be the accuser. I had to eventually stand up and shout out, "Satan, No weapon formed against us shall prosper. You couldn't take my mind in 2009 and you won't do it now. God has not forsaken us. We have ministering angels encamped all around us. My husband is just fine and my son is fine, as well. We will come through this also. You still lose!" I immediately began to worship the Father and the satanic forces from hell and voices hushed. What a Mighty God we serve!

As I stated before, I had to choose between my husband coming home or my son. I'm not sure what anyone else might have done, but for me it was a "no brainer". My husband was only trying to keep order in our house against a 17 year old child trying to take over. I stood with him all of the way. I witnessed the compassion, the sacrifices and attempts, to reason with our son in order to reach him. The more we gave, the more he demanded without any giving on his part. We realized that our son needed some intervention naturally. We covered all bases spiritually. We needed the system to take him out of our house in order to get the help he needed. It was not our son who didn't want to be around us, but the unclean spirit. He wouldn't leave. The spirit's assignment was to stay near us just to aggravate us, through his rebelling. Our son tried to manipulate us into giving him things, not realizing that he was opening the doors for satanic attacks. His assignment was to be our distraction from ministry. The Lord spoke to one of our pastor friends, using the term that all that had occurred was "back lash" from hell because of our seeking the Father and casting him out of other vessels.

The way it all went was not at all what we expected, but as I mentioned in a previous chapter, the process of deliverance is not left up to us. Our prayer was for our son to get some needed help. The good news is, he is now getting that. We pray daily for all of our children and therefore we are convinced that they will all come into the destiny of salvation. Parents, what we see, our children's actions, is only temporal therefore subject to change. God's Word is eternal in the heavens. God cannot lie. Saints, stay encouraged and as pertaining to our children, look out for book #3. We will shout together about what Jesse, my other three children and my grandson Jeremiah, will be doing in the ministry, if Christ should tarry.

Chapter VIII

Anointed in Your Living, Giving and Worship

When one desires to be anointed of God, you must live right. That means no longer living as to yourself. You must submit your will to God. As you grow in your relationship with Him you will find that this becomes easier to do. One will begin to yield more quickly to the Spirit of God than to your flesh. The bible says, "You must come from among them and be separate; touch not the unclean things of the world. And God said then, I will be unto you a Father and you will be my sons and daughters, saith the Lord Almighty" (2 Corinthians 6:16 &17).

Our desire should be to always represent Christ in our conduct and appearance. One can not dress like the world (tight and revealing). **Ladies, you must be appealing not revealing**. There is a difference. Please allow me to say this here; there was a time we as women dared not to wear certain types of clothing into the house of God. That is not the case now. There are women who come to church dress as if they are going to a night club or a picnic with no modesty. We make it hard for men to keep their eyes on the preacher while in service. There was a time when men had to go to the night club to see sexual attire, but now we bring all of that into God's house. Ladies, God is not pleased. Remember, you will get what you advertise for. You must encourage men to be **attracted to your inner beauty, not your flesh. Your flesh will not stay the same over time.** It changes. If a man is drawn to your Christ like characteristics, a meek and quiet spirit, you have a better chance of having a lasting relationship. Don't be so caught up in how he dresses or where he works or lives. That same good looking, well-dressed, smooth talking, religious man can turn out to be your worst nightmare once he gets you alone.

To the men, there was a time when you dared not to approach a woman inappropriately in church. Now you think as long as the preacher does not hear or see you, you are safe. Just know the pastor does not have the keys to death, hell nor heaven but your sins will find you out. Remember, these are God's children and when you mistreat or disrespect them or God's place of worship you fall into the hands of an angry God.

When our ministry began exposing the enemy from the pulpit in these two areas, dress and motives, some in our local congregation fell away. We have been given a mandate from the father though; we have to preach against seducing spirits released in the church. Yes, Jesus did say "Come as you are", but you are to be taught. Once you have been taught better, you are expected to do better. The scripture states, if eating meat will cause my brother to stumble, I will reframe" I Corinthians 8:13. This is in comparative to if dressing provocative will cause my brother in the Lord to stumble or sin, I will reframe.

You must have a standard of living to be anointed. Not only do you live by the standard but you must also be willing to expose the enemy, no matter the costs. I am convinced the reason that so many marriages fail is because husband and wife are drawn to each other for the wrong reasons, looks and material possessions. Both are temporal and therefore subject to change. Health fails and possessions can be taken away, but a man or woman with a converted spirit is eternal.

A word to the singles, seek first to know if that individual has a relationship with Jesus Christ, not religion. There is a major difference. Religion will cause them to treat you right on Sunday during the eleven o clock hour only a show before others, legalism. But a relationship with Christ will cause them to treat you right all day every day. It will be a lifestyle before the father, because He is watching.

Singles, called to possess their vessels

(1) Ladies, if you would learn to stop discounting your merchandise, the buyer would take better care of it.
(2) Stop lowering your standards for acceptance.
(3) A man goes into a specialty shop expecting to pay more. Let him know the value of your goods is more than an occasional

date in secret or a text. You can't be found on the bargain or clearance rack.

(4) You have a commitment price tag on your goods. Fellas, you've got to put a ring on it. And women stop fooling yourself saying, "You don't want a committed relationship, you don't want to be married again". No, what you are saying is, you don't want to be hurt again. Everybody wants somebody to call their own.

(5) Singles, shacking is not an alternate lifestyle for Christians, but for sinners. Marriage is God's way.

Your Giving Reflects Your Living

You must give right to be anointed. God began to show me that His people will trust Him with just about everything but their money. "Give, and it shall be given unto you; good measure, pressed down, and shaken together, and running over, shall men give into your bosom. For with the same measure that ye mete withal it shall be measured to you again" (Luke 6:38).

A deception of the adversary is for God's people to limit how much we are willing to obey when it comes to our giving. Anointed people seek opportunities to sow. "For where your treasure is, there will your heart be also" (Matthew 6:21). T. D. Jakes cloned a phrase, "We dress better than we give, we shout better than we live. Our talk in church, don't match our walk outside the church." The naked truth is God must be Lord over your finances and material goods:"Bring ye all the tithes into the storehouse, that there may be meat in mine house" (Malachi 3:10). A tithe is a tenth of your substance.

In bible study one Wednesday, a member asked, "Is a tithe limited to ten percent?" We explained that the minimum would be the ten percent. Tithing was included under the law but not restricted to it. What we mean by that is once we accept Jesus Christ as our Savior and Lord one could never give too much. We understand that the whole one hundred percent belongs to Him but He trusts us to be the manager of it. He asks us to prove Him. Give Him back ten percent, sow it into your local church and you keep the ninety percent. Watch how he multiplies the ninety percent because of your obedience. He reminds us that the more we trust him to return back to us, the more we should give.

Have you ever heard of an individual that went to a restaurant and ordered from the menu, ate good and instead of paying the bill, just left the waitress a tip? That's how many people handle God's business. They come to church, eat good spiritually and instead of paying for the meal (tithes) they leave a tip. We should give in proportion to our trust in Him. To obey is better than sacrifice. I Samuel 15:22

Anointed Worship

Worship is not limited to a position of the body, but a condition of the body, spirit and soul. The word of God states that we know that God hears not sinner's prayers, but if any man be a worshipper of God, him will He hear. Your worship creates an atmosphere that celebrates the presence of God. Worship is not an emotion, it is a lifestyle, "The Father seeketh such to worship Him in spirit and truth" (John 4:4). All men can praise God, but only those who have had a born again encounter with Him can worship Him. We praise Him with our body , but we worship Him with our born again spirit and our obedience to His Word.

Worship is our outward expression of our excessive love for our heavenly Father. It is our gratitude through obedience. He said "If ye love me, keep my commandments" (John 14:15). He also said it is a vain statement of worship if you bow privately but publically you won't obey me. That's religion and it is in vain:"If a man say, I love God, and hateth his brother, he is a liar; for he that loveth not his brother whom he hath seen, how can he love God whom he hath not seen? And this commandment have we from him, That he who loveth God loves his brother also"

(1 John 4:20-21)

To be anointed requires great sacrificial love to all mankind, especially to those of the household of faith… Christians. You will not be able to love your fellow Christians like this until you are in relationship with the father and His spirit indwells you. Love comes from God because God is love. Unconditional love births the anointing."Beloved, let us love one another:. For love is of God and every one that loveth is born of God, and knoweth God. He that loveth not knoweth not God for God is love"(I John 4:7-8). "No greater love than this for a man to lay down his life for his friend" (John 15:13).

Chapter IX

Anointed to Preach, Called to Pastor

*A*nointed pastors, pastor hurting people: "When Jesus heard that, he said unto them, They that be whole need not a physician, but they that are sick" (Matthew 9:12). "How God anointed Jesus of Nazareth with the Holy Ghost and with power: who went about doing good, and healing all that were oppressed of the devil; for God was with him" (Acts 10:38).

God even anointed his son Jesus to preach. He prepared Him for ministry, first through equipping Him with the Holy Ghost and with power. He charged Him first to live right and treat folks right, according to the Word of God. Afterwards, to go on to do the work of the ministry; healing the sick and delivering those who were oppressed by evil spirits. He assured Him that God was with Him. Christ is to be our example. After thirty years of ministry, my husband and I have come to know the importance of being assured that God is with us in ministry.

Pastoring people is a calling that you have to make your election sure of: "Wherefore the rather, brethren, give diligence to make your calling and election sure; for if ye do these things, ye shall never fall" (II Peter 1:10). For every true man and woman that has been called to minister by God, there will come a time of serious testing. It will not matter how long you have stayed the course. A fork will appear in the road, and when that time comes one must know that he knows that this is what he has been called and ordained to do. One must know that God is with him because just saying, "I heard a voice," won't be enough to cause you to continue in ministry.

In 1 Samuel 3:6, the Lord was calling Samuel into ministry. Samuel did not yet know the voice of the Lord so he immediately went to his mentor, his teacher, Eli and asked him did he call him. God calls Samuel again and Samuel responds the same way, by going to Eli. Until a person can identify the voice of God, they limit God's voice to that of their pastor or teacher, "Again, he arose and went to Eli, and said, Here am I; for thou didst call me. And Eli perceived that the Lord had called the child. Therefore Eli said to Samuel, Go, lie down, and it shall be, if he call thee, that thou shall say, Speak, Lord; for thy servant heareth" (I Samuel 3:8-9).

Notice Eli didn't instruct Samuel to "go preach" because he heard somebody call his name. He told him yes, I believe the Lord has called you, but we need to make your calling and election sure. So go lay back down (today's instructions would be, go fast and pray) and if it's a true calling, it will come with instructions.

God knew that for Samuel to stay faithful to his assignment, he had to be convinced that it came from Him. God also knows even today for His pastors to obey Him rather than man, we have to know who we are employed by, who signs the check. We have to know that it is not the man, nor the job, not even the seemed appointee. They may be our resource but never our source. God will not share His glory nor credit with a human being. God supplies (source) all our needs. He usually accomplishes this through man but sometimes by supernatural means.

Pastors are employees of God, not of man, not of the deacon board, nor of an organization. We have to indeed be fully convinced of this. Our assignment is to the people of God. Pastors are given to the people as a gift, but most of the time, many of the people don't have a true appreciation for the set man or woman of God. If you are not a hireling and can't be controlled, seduced, manipulated or intimidated, you will not be very popular with those in the congregation that are unconverted. The spirit of Jezebel released in the church will cause those who you pray, fast and counsel with the most to be the first to deny you. As long as you are acknowledging their works and turning your head to their sins, they praise you for being the most committed pastor in the city. They will say they feel the anointing every Sunday, Wednesday and even when they drive by the church, (a little humor). My pastor can do no wrong. But the moment you bring about a correction in their life, they cry out "crucify him/her!" We should not want shepherds who will only tell us what we want to hear. True shepherds tell the sheep what they need to hear as well. We all have blind spots. Those are spots that we need help seeing. Because we are so close to the object we can't objectively see them, so others may have to bring it to our attention. That's the purpose of a true shepherd.

"All scripture is given by inspiration of God, and is profitable for doctrine, for reproof, for correction, for instruction in righteousness" (II Timothy 3:16). Our Pastor's words and/or hands not only soothe and comfort us, but in other cases that same voice or hand must correct, and sometimes pain is felt. A true sheep, not goat will receive the correction as well as the smoothing strokes, but those which are not of the fold will buck correction and will find fault in the pastor. When offended, that spirit of the antichrist will enter in through the spirit of offense (spirit of error, sent to "off, end" the process and plan of God). A true son does not despise the chastening or correction from the word of God but being stubborn and unteachable allows Satan to enter into an individual's thought life.

Satan immediately seeds you with lies or deception in order to steal your peace. He will convince you that you are not growing spiritually. He will get your mind off the word while sitting in the service and magnify everything else around you. He will make you feel out of place. All of a sudden there's no love in the church. There are clicks in the church. Pastor is acting indifferent toward you. Pastor only allows certain people to do things in the church and the fault finding list goes on and on in the mind.

God revealed to me that the enemy in them is not against the pastor personally, but against the anointing that's upon his/her life. This is why one must truly be anointed to pastor, to be equipped to "love the hell" out of them, and that's for real. People will push you to the limit. A pastor must love in spite of, not because of, must be able to discern the spirit from an individual's flesh. They have to remind themselves that we do not wrestle against flesh and blood but against principalities and powers and rulers of darkness in high places. Jesus told Peter, "Get behind me Satan" (Matthew 16:23). He was not talking to the man Peter, but the spirit that was speaking through him at the time. Pastors must be able to rightly discern the spirit that is using any laymen at any given time.

Satan's assignment is to bring discord among the body, to stop growth, to bring discouragement to the man or woman of God. He is mainly a distraction. If the spirit behind the individual can't stop the plan of God, they are to attempt to delay its occurrence. We have had individuals sent into our midst with the assignment to "kill, steal and destroy". They have come in with witchcraft spirits; attempting to control the service, trying to manipulate other members. These individuals, in their mind, often have a word from the Lord for others, but never realizing that word was probably for them.

We thank God for keeping us through prayer and giving us discernment because though the weapons formed, they did not prosper. God would show us who Satan was using in the service and yet, He would instruct us to love them regardless. Some would come and say Pastor I love you and I am with you and all the time we knew they were operating in seducing and controlling spirits. Satan will even plant people in your local church to try to bring division between the Pastor and the Assistant or Board of Elders. We had a case where the individual went so far as to tell the Apostle that he felt if he only had a male, instead of a female, being the Assistant Pastor, the church would grow more. They were in error, not knowing the scriptures for Galatians 3:28 states there is neither bond nor free, there is neither male nor female; for ye are all one in Jesus Christ (the anointing). So it is not the sex of the individual that increases or stunts the growth but the obedience of the individual to the word of God. The Bible states in Proverbs, "Even a fool, when he holdeth his peace, is counted wise: *and* he that shutteth his lips *is esteemed* a man of understanding" (Proverbs 17:28).

We immediately knew this message was not of God nor were they; because the word tells us they God added to the church such as should be save. They failed to realize that this appointment was the Lords doing and it is marvelous in both of our sight.

Satan hates the union of marriage between one man and one woman, and triples the amount when there is marriage and ministry under one roof. It's because there is a balance that occurs in ministry. Whenever my husband and I counsel other pastors, we encourage them to use wisdom when it comes to ministering. The easiest part of ministry is standing in the pulpit and delivering a message from the Lord. True testing can come in the one-on-one counseling sessions between a male pastor and a female member or a female Pastor with a male member. Even in counseling, we cannot give any place to our adversary, if we want to be anointed. There will be some hurting people that are sent to your ministry to receive healing and wholeness from the Lord. One must be wise as a serpent yet harmless as a dove when dealing with the opposite sex. To avoid potential pitfalls, there should be another Minister present when a male is counseling a female or a female is counseling with a male. This structure doesn't leave room to give place for deception. God calls us to be helpmeets to our spouses in more than just the home.

Satan will use people in any means to bring division. Some will claim to want to get close to the apostle or pastor to help them but their agenda is to get information to use against them just as Delilah did Samson in Judges. Pastors must avoid the spirit of familiarity with the sheep. God will give you the spirit of discernment to determine what their motives are. He will not allow you to be caught by surprise. He will instruct you to continue to pastor and love all your flock, even those that mean you no good. It definitely takes the anointing of the father to "love those who despitefully use you and say all manner of evil against you falsely" (Matthew 5:12).

Once Satan knows that you have passed the love or forgiveness test with the congregation his last resort, a spirit of deception, will enter in through offense. Satan will cause them to leave the church and sometimes carry other innocent and naïve individuals with them. He convinces the individual to go ahead and leave the church with thoughts such as, "you will show that pastor that they need you and that the people look up to you" but they don't see the big picture. What Satan is really after is their soul. If he can't destroy the ministry through them then he would still get some gratification from just getting him or her to "self destruct". He would do this through isolation or even an unscheduled transfer, to move you from your set place without authorization. Satan will have you convinced that through this move you are happier now.

You will try to justify your move. You now are made to feel that the air is fresher in your new church although, mind you, it is in the same part of town. You now say there is no division at your new church; your new pastor is perfect. He or She recognizes your anointing. You can tell you are going to be in leadership here very soon. God showed you that this is where you needed to be all the time. So either God has Alzheimer's or schizophrenia because you said God told you to join the last church you left. That is interesting to say the least.

There is one main problem, God stops speaking at your last place of disobedience. One must discern whose voice it is they are hearing and obeying. Many times once the individual gets settled in at their new place of worship, the same old offense presents itself. The best thing one can do is stop the cycle and repent. Whatever has offended you is a spot that God is working on. Repent and be converted (changed and delivered) before your time of refreshing (visitation).

In most cases, those who have the spirit of Christ, those who are of Him will recognize the error of their ways and repent and return to their church home. You should always welcome them back and continue to teach and preach the truth of God's word to the congregation. It is God's word that brings about deliverance. God can anoint anyone

He chooses, but ultimately, He is the source of deliverance. Ministry is all about a Father that loved the world so much that He provided a way for us all to return to Him.

We as ministers, have a responsibility to share the word and love of God with those that do not know about it or understand it. We are His mouthpiece in the earth. We are "laborers together with God" (I Corinthians 3:9). When He entrusts you enough to bestow upon you His precious anointing, be sure that you operate in syncopation with Him at all times. He runs the show and will direct you every step of the way. Always remember that the people belong to God. You are an under shepherd, but He is the "...chief Shepherd..."(I Peter 5:4) and if you ever get out of line, God will hold you accountable. Ezekiel 34:1-5 And the Word of the Lord came unto me saying, Son of man, prophesy against the shepherds of Israel, prophesy, and say unto them Thus saith the Lord God unto the shepherds; Woe (Warnings) be to the shepherds of Israel that do feed themselves! Should not the shepherds feed the flocks? Ye eat the fat, and ye clothe you with the wool, ye kill them that are fed: But ye feed not the flock. The diseased have ye not strengthen, neither have ye healed that which was sick, neither have ye bound up that which was broken, neither have ye brought again that which was driven away, neither have ye sought that which was lost; but with force and with cruelty have ye ruled them. And they were scattered, because there is no shepherd; and they became meat to all the beasts of the field, when they were scattered.

So, You Want to Be Anointed?

Pastors and five fold, Everything that is "presented is not for the possession". It can be a setup, flee fornication, as with Joseph (Genesis 39:12). Things that are pleasing to the five senses, can be in opposition to the Spirit of God. When you are not Anointed you are not equipped for ministry, to properly lead, instruct, cover and care for God's People and therefore we misuse God's elect. As disobedient and rebellious as we all can be, God loves us and He knows how to deal with us individually. As you seek the anointing of God, test your motives and be sure your desire is to glorify God. We are anointed for ministry. Our ministry is people. Our mandate is to set the captive free, through the preaching of Jesus death, burial and resurrection. We can fulfill our assignment through the anointing. The Holy Ghost will give you the power to just say "No", If you want to be Anointed and let the Power of God show. Get Anointed!

As disobedient and rebellious as we can all be, God loves us and He knows how to deal with us individually. As you seek the anointing of God, test your motives and be sure your desire is to glorify God.

We are anointed for ministry. Our ministry is people. Our mandate is to set the captive free. We can fulfill our assignment through the anointing.

Chapter X

To Be or Not to Be Anointed?

Advantages of Being Anointed	Disadvantages of Not Being Anointed
You come to know God in the power of His resurrection and in the fellowship of His suffering.	You have limited power. You are a thirty-fold believer (Matthew 13:23), you make the confession without the possession.
You receive power to endure or to hold up under extreme circumstances.	You are saved, but you are defeated in everyday living. There is no consistent joy or peace.
You are bold and confident in the God of your salvation.	You are intimidated and fearful by the report of your adversary.
You are not ashamed of the gospel of Jesus Christ. Your life represents change.	You become double minded. You go with the flow. One day you confess God can do anything. The very next day you operate in fear and unbelief.
Your adversary recognizes your authority through Jesus Christ.	You will fall for the set-up and traps of the adversary through deception.
You will have supernatural faith.	You will not have steadfast, unmovable faith.
Your sons and your daughters shall prophesy and your older men shall dream dreams and your young men shall see visions	You can only see your present state of being. You are limited in your vision, you can't call things that be not as though they were.

Chapter XI

Commonly Asked Questions about the Anointing

1. **Can you be a Christian and not be Anointed?**

   Yes. As compared to you can be a Believer without being Filled with the Holy Spirit.

2. **What is the major difference between being filled with the Holy Spirit and the Anointing?**

   The Holy Spirit comes upon and in you by asking for Him according to Luke 11:9. The Anointing is received after the crushing, being conformed to God's image after dying to the flesh.

3. **Can a person lose their anointing?**

   Yes. You can forfeit God's approval or His presence through character flaws. God won't live in an unclean vessel. You can lose your anointing as you can lose your salvation. God never lets go of us, but we let go of Him to grab hold of the world.

4. **Is the anointing for all denominations; what if I am a Baptist, Methodist or Presbyterian?**

The relevant question would be, are you a believer? Man devised denominations. God made spirits. He sees His spirit with free course in our vessels. So once you receive Jesus, get filled with His Presence, then the anointing is made available to you.

5. **I have been praying for more of Jesus. I want to be ready when He returns to the earth. I don't feel I am doing all I have been put here to do. I am save, filled But I want to do more to help people. Will the Anointing equip me?**

Yes; the Anointing will stretch you pass your limit to your ability.

6. **If I am in ministry (Pastoring or Evangelizing) and I seem to be at a plateau in my ministry, a burnout, how can the Anointing help me to become more engaged? I admit I need something more, greater, not horizontal (not something without, but something within). Not another church engagement, not another revival where nothing changes, people shout, people cry, people rejoice for the moment then business as usual. I need a vertical inreach. Can the anointing help my ministry?**

Absolutely. More importantly, the anointing will help you. The burnout could indicate that you have been doing all the work instead of the Holy Spirit. As you die to your own desires and works, the crushing of your will causes the oil (the scent, the fragrance) of His presence to come upon and you. The potter sometimes splatters the clay, to make the vessel all over again and causes it to then be displayed as a trophy to the world.

Conclusion

When God put it in my Spirit to write this book, I knew it would not come without a spiritual fight. I knew that the Holy Spirit would have to put me under the "witness protection" surveillance. He has done just that and we win. Satan has definitely tried to "turn it up" with the warfare, but we have seen God stand up on our behalf, mightily.

In conclusion, being anointed is a good thing, but keep in mind it comes with a cost. Just as Jesus was anointed, we too must be anointed; however, we must understand its purpose. The anointing is for deliverance, healing, and endurance. It is given to aid, support, and build up others in their desire to know Christ and be a part of His kingdom. The Bible records, "many are the afflictions of the righteous but God delivers him out of them all" (Psalms 34:19). It also says comfort ye one another" (I Thessalonians 5:11a). The end result is to be as compassionate toward others as Jesus is.

Being anointed is a lonely walk, but not a lonesome one. The higher you go up the fewer the number that follows. Many that say,

"Pastor I am with you for the long haul and I will never deny or betray you" will leave you in your most vulnerable hour. The spirit that came upon Peter to deny and Judas to betray will show up in those closest to you. Even when you know your Peter and Judas, you are sometimes still instructed to allow them to walk with you until their deliverance takes place. That process is working a greater weight of glory in both. Many times we choose to opt out of the line of fire, but that is where the anointing is made known. In the process we are made in the image and likeness of Jesus, unconditional love. Image is defined as; a likeness, appearance, representation of someone, similarity. So while being tested in our love walk or endurance we are made in an appearance, a form similar to Jesus. We have the ability to love as He loves, to live as He lived, to overcome the world, to have joy and peace in the Holy Ghost:

> And there was delivered unto Him the book of the prophet Esaias. And when he had opened the Book, he found the place where it was written, The Spirit of the Lord is upon me, because he has anointed me to preach the gospel to the poor, he hath sent me to heal the brokenhearted, to preach deliverance to the captives, and recovering of sight to the blind, to set at liberty them that are bruised, To preach the acceptable year of the Lord. And he closed the book, and he gave it again to the minister, and sat down. And the eyes of all them that were in the synagogue were fastened

on him. And he began to say unto them, This Day is this scripture fulfilled in your ears. (Luke 4:17-21)

There is no anointing without a fight. There's no anointing without being wounded. The crushing releases the oil. Then the oil, which represents His presence, is smeared through the body. So don't run from the making; engage the fight through the word and remember, the reward far outweighs the test. Just know that life is just the reenactment of where our faith has already been. Get in agreement with your spirit man concerning the outcome and just know because of your endurance through testing and trials like a good soldier, your anointing is made "authentic". The anointing should be the apex of every Believers Desire. We Win!

Contact Information

If you would like more information about the author for speaking engagements or seminars or more information on the ministries, you may contact them at:

Pastor P. J. Taylor

HIS WORD Ministries (Church)

1200 20th Street North

Birmingham, AL 35234

H.E.R.S. Womens Ministries

(Honoring Every Resurrected Sister)

herspt@aol.com

OR <u>mwtpjt@aol.com</u>
OR <u>hiswordministry@bellsouth.net</u>
<u>PHONE 205 531-0081 OR 531-1908</u>

www.ingramcontent.com/pod-product-compliance
Lightning Source LLC
LaVergne TN
LVHW022000060526
838201LV00048B/1641